THE ULTIMATE
GUIDE FOR ELEVATION TO THE

NEXLEVEL

Hebrews 3: 6-11
4: 1-10

THE ULTIMATE
GUIDE FOR ELEVATION TO THE

NEXLEVEL

RAMONE PRESTON

TABLE OF CONTENTS

Acknowledgments

Introduction

ACKNOWLEDGMENTS

First & Foremost, I'm eternally indebted to my Lord, my Savior, my Everything, Jesus Christ! Without Him there is no me, period! Secondly, to my best friend, my partner in life, my beautiful wife, Dione Preston! You keep me grounded, you keep me happy, and I'm more in love with you today than I was when I first laid my eyes on you.

To my babies, Ramani Preston (Tai'lyn), and Ramone Preston Jr. Outside of being saved and being a husband, there's no greater accomplishment in life than being your daddy (Papa) and I love you with all of my heart!

To the current Matriarch of our family, my sister Kellie Clancy and the entire "Clancy Clan", Shivaun, Britany, Jamarion, Javon, Janai, & Javeah! To all my siblings, my family members, my in-laws, and my friends, I thank you so much for loving and supporting me.

To my Mother in Love, my Mothers & Fathers in the faith, my spiritual covering, and most certainly, my KHOM family, I'm so humbled & honored that you allow me to do life with you.

To my late Father and Mother, Howard and Charlene Preston, who gave birth to me, and who died confidently knowing that I would keep their legacy alive.

Finally, to my late grandmother, Johanne Clancy, who loved me, raised me, groomed me, and gave me everything I needed to be the man I am today.

INTRODUCTION

As far back as I can possibly remember, I have always possessed unusual desires and dreams to be more, to do more, to have more, and to see more. During the few rare occasions as a child, that I was fortunate to visit Manhattan, New York, I would literally be in awe just gazing at the skylines, the high-rises, and all the bright lights in the City!

The story of my life proves that this whole idea of "The NexLevel", is not some unusual phenomena that only happens to a few extraordinary people. The truth is that, God plants into the DNA of every human being, the desires and dreams for Elevation to the NexLevel.

The challenge, however, is for you to be positioned at some point in your life, around the right people who can help expose you to the truth about NexLevel Living. Despite your age, your race, or your wages, God is an equal opportunity provider for those who are willing and ready to experience NexLevel Living. Acts 10:34 says, *"God does not show partiality or favoritism".* In other words, there is always a place exclusively designated in the NexLevel for you.

At this point in my life, there is nothing more gratifying to me than to know that my contribution to the world is helping others experience fulfillment in their lives. As a matter of fact, I believe when God graces you with the self-awareness, the empathy, the compassion, and the capacity to connect with people, that He also holds you accountable to help them get to the NexLevel.

That is why I'm so thankful to God. The blessing of this book allows me to publicate and articulate a personal process that I've been able to successfully live through.

My hope and expectation is: The revelation that exists within the framework of this book, will inspire you, activate you, and ultimately guide you, to your elevated place in the NexLevel!

Humbly,

Ramone Preston

CHAPTER 1

PREPARATION FOR ELEVATION

Romans 12:2

And do not be conformed to this world, but be transformed by the renewing of your mind, that you may prove what is that good and acceptable and perfect will of God.

One of the most amazing discoveries you will ever make in your life, is the discovery of who you actually are on the inside. Social experts refer to this discovery as self-awareness, which suggests that you possess a unique comfort in the true you and an unmatched capacity for what you do.

The Greek word for this discovery is metamorphosis, which refers to a process that leads to the progressive, permanent change in your life. This discovery process is a very important aspect of your preparation for elevation because it's only when you change or morph your mind, that you will be able to change or morph your Life!

If you never change your mind about your elevation, you will never shape your life for elevation. This is why so many people live their entire lives on the bottom and never experience their best life on the top.

At some point in your life there has to be a renewing of your mind that subsequently transforms you beyond living in a place that is good or acceptable, and ultimately into a place that perfectly positions you for NexLevel living!

What Is Elevation?

Elevation simply means the height above a given level. The origination of this word has close ties with the two English words "lever and elevator". Together these words carry the idea of bringing something down so it can take someone up. In order for elevation to exist, there has to be a foundation or a basis from which something or someone can be heightened and taken up. In other words, if there is no bottom in your life, there can be no top for your life. This is why the idea of elevation speaks such volumes to why you have to appreciate small beginnings.

Everything you endeavor to do spiritually, socially, financially, and economically requires a bottom or a basis. Every bottom or basis has to be built on the proper assessment of how high that endeavor has the potential to go up to. This is why it's absolutely imperative to build every area of your life on the foundation of God's perfect will. Otherwise the world will conform you or morph you into their flawed definition of you.

When you are willing to accept the perfect blueprint God wants to establish for your elevated life, the battles you face on the bottom won't break you, God will use them to ultimately bless you. Once your beginning or basis is established, you have a much better chance of going up and staying up. It doesn't matter how long this foundational process takes or how tough it gets. You will always find peace in knowing that your beginning is just a basis for your elevation!

3 THINGS YOUR ELEVATION REQUIRES

Now that you have a clear working definition and description for what elevation is and how elevation works in your life, it's equally important for you to understand the three things your elevation requires.

1. Your Elevation Requires Saturation

The purpose of saturation is to soak, impregnate, and furnish your spirit with the truth about your elevation. This soaking allows you to possess the capacity to live in the manifestation of what God promised you, once you get to where he's taking you. Just because God has called you to elevation doesn't necessarily mean you have the spiritual capacity to experience elevation. This is why saturation is never a request from God, but a requirement by God.

Sometimes people want God to transform them spiritually, when God wants to first renew them mentally. I know this may sound kind of counterproductive to our understanding of spirituals things, but the truth is, most of the things God does for you are based on what you already set in your mind for Him to do. At some point in the process of God doing some spiritual thing in your life, you made it up in your mind that you actually wanted Him to do it. Once that mental decision was made by you, the spiritual experience was then executed by God.

For this very reason you should never downplay or dismiss the importance of the role that your mind plays in the saturation that God uses to furnish your spirit with the truth about your elevation. It is also important to note that during your required season of saturation God will cause you to be drenched with situational storms designed to discipline you, develop you, mentor you, and mature you for the elevated place He's prepared for you.

2. Your Elevation Requires Separation

The purpose of separation is not just to pull you apart from what you believed in your past, but it also poises you for how to behave in your present. The origination of the word separation carries the idea of pulling you apart for the purpose of making you ready. There are so many people who believe what they believe because of what other people programmed them to believe. Social experts refer to this as "environmental determinism", which simply means that you believe, behave and become what you're always around.

It's impossible to change your behavior, if you never change your beliefs. It's equally impossible to change your beliefs if you don't change your surroundings and your sources of information. This is exactly why God uses the saturation of present truth to separate you from the trauma of past lies. Everything we go through in life is instrumental in shaping our thoughts, ideas, beliefs, and our philosophies about how far we can go and how high we can soar. You will never rise above your level of revelation or the truth about your elevation.

The Bible says when we know the truth, it will set us free. The operative word here is "know", which suggests that we must become intimately acquainted with what God intends for us to do and where He imagines us to go. This divine impartation of revelation about your elevation requires total separation from any person, any place, or anything that doesn't assist you in your Elevation to the NexLevel.

Although separation can be a very hard process for you and for those that are connected to you. It is a necessary experience for God to show you exactly who's fixed on your past and who's focused on your future. If people are with you and for you, they will understand God's separation of you.

3. Your Elevation Requires Acceleration

The purpose of acceleration is to cause faster, greater velocity and activity in your mind, in order to increase speed and reduce time in your life. This word carries the idea of positive progressions without pauses. In other words, acceleration not only speeds your destiny up, but it simultaneously shuts your delays down. This is where you start moving at the pace of your purpose and living at the speed of your obedience. It's very important to understand the correlation of both pace and speed, because your purpose in God and your obedience to God totally depend on it. You can't have one without the other and they must become complimentary to the momentum that your required acceleration has produced for you.

As a matter of fact, at this stage of your preparation, you can't afford to entertain anyone or anything that could potentially slow down your process of elevation to the NexLevel. If people didn't grow with you during your season of saturation and separation, then unfortunately they can't go with you in your season of acceleration. According to Ephesians 5:16, once you've been saturated and separated, you have a biblical blessing to redeem your time and make the most of your time by allowing God to accelerate you into a deeper dimension of your destiny.

This supernatural dynamic transcends time and gives you access to the speed of eternity, which is needed to continue scaling you in and through each NexLevel God elevates you to. You are also responsible for not becoming intoxicated in the idea of moving so fast. Just because people are making good moves doesn't mean they're making the right moves. Steer clear of those things that keep you extremely busy but never hold you accountable for handling your business.

CHAPTER 2

4 PHASES OF ELEVATION

Acts 1:9

And after He said these things, He was caught up as they looked on, and a cloud took Him up out of their sight.

Despite all the studies and statistics that support the safety and security of flying on aircrafts, there are still countless individuals who will never venture near an airport. Most of them are afraid of heights. They are terrified of flying because of bad information and observations, not from an actual flying experience.

This is the very reason why Jesus invested 3½ years preparing His disciples for elevation to the NexLevel. He walked with them, talked with them, and always referenced the importance of going up. Jesus illustrated a "gateway" with His prophetic promise as recorded in John 12:32. He said, *"when I am lifted up from the earth, I will draw all men unto me"*!

In order to successfully navigate to the NexLevel in any area of your life, you should have a vested interest in the proper information and observations that support your NexLevel experience. Which means you have to walk with and talk with individuals who can properly guide you during your "pilot" season of teaching and training. Once you have been adequately prepared for your flight, you are now ready to "rip the runway" for Elevation to the NexLevel.

1. The Takeoff Phase

This is the pre-flight phase that you must use to evaluate what's at your gate and look to see who's around your ground. By now you should have already checked-in any baggage that was too heavy for you to carry on board. Sometimes we can become so inundated in celebrating the fact that we're going places in certain areas of our life that we don't realize we're bringing extra luggage and unauthorized items on board with us.

Although most people who are passengers to our purpose don't like the wait at the gate, it is however, a very important part of the process to qualify everyone for your flight. One of the first things you're instructed to do at takeoff is to stay seated and strapped while the aircraft is elevating, because of the friction and discomfort that the takeoff creates. They also warn you that one bad decision can potentially ground the aircraft and consequently cause you to be banned for life.

This is exactly why we must stay positioned and poised when God begins to elevate us in life, in ministry, or even in business. God wants your ground level training to hold you together once you begin to fly high. If you allow old baggage and other devices to manipulate you into making bad decisions during your takeoff, what God wanted to use to groom you, the enemy will use to ground you!

2. The Climb Phase

The climbing phase of your flight is when everything looks dark and everyone is silent. This is a crucial part of your process because all of the energy is being used to push the aircraft to a predetermined level. Experts suggest that in a successful climb, the volume of "excess thrust" is determined by the force from the power plant that must exceed the drag on the aircraft. All available energy has to be used to defy the laws of gravity that wants to force the aircraft back to the ground. Whatever God is elevating you to, will determine how much time and energy you need to invest in order to get your vision off the ground. You can't expect God to give you something or take you somewhere you're unwilling to sacrifice everything for. You must also be willing to do whatever is necessary without having a clear point of reference. Why? Because the greatest things are seen in the darkest times of your life, and the best things are heard when everyone stops talking.

3. The Cruise Phase

This is the phase of your flight when everyone and everything "Levels-Up" after the climb to a set altitude. It is at this point in your life, your ministry, or your business that you realize everyone presently with you is headed in the same direction. This is a very gratifying moment of rest and relief because most people never reach this altitude. For those who do, enjoy all the luxuries and embrace all the amenities that are now afforded at this phase of their flight. You deserve the amenities of this phase!

Some of the luxuries and amenities include being able to walk around without regulations. This reflects your ability to discern that although you're not where you want to be, you still have a healthy appreciation for where you are, simply because you're not where you used to be. You also have the freedom to use your wireless devices, watch movies, play games, and even eat a decent meal. This reflects your balanced approach to NexLevel living because you never want to be all work and no play.

I highly recommend that you absorb every moment of this phase, because too many people are found guilty being so focused on how they fought to get there, that they forget to celebrate the favor they have now that they are there. Whenever you face the temptation to resist this restful, relaxing phase of your life, remember that the cruise phase usually consumes the majority of a flight. You should never be disturbed by the possibility of periodic turbulence.

4. The Landing Phase

This is the final phase of your flight that safely brings you to your predetermined elevated place. You should be well rounded, rested, relieved, and ready to make your miraculous landing. Whether your phases took days, weeks, months, or even years, you cannot allow the process to cloud your judgment. You must maintain a clear vision for this elevated place that you're approaching. Your job, your marriage, your ministry, your business, your degree, your family, and everything else that you paid the price in the process of your flight to receive will be awaiting you upon your arrival!

Let me caution you because although this is the final phase of your flight and you're about to make a landing, you still have many potential risks that you must be mindful of. There are crosswinds, holding patterns, and other delayed flights ahead that God will interject into your scheduled arrival just to see if you've learned to turn your losses into lessons and your past fights into your future favors. This will be an important moment during your descent because your life can't land in that elevated place until the coast is clear. So while you're descending, be sure to clear the runway of your heart so no detrimental debris will show up in your life.

CHAPTER 3

LIVING FROM AN ELEVATED PLACE

Ezekiel 37:12

I will open your graves and cause you to come up…

One of the biggest mistakes that you can make is to believe that since God has blessed you with a changed mind, He's also eliminated every problem from your life. This fabrication of truth will form unrealistic expectations in your heart that will drive you back to baggage claim trying to pick up things you shouldn't even have in your life.

The truth is that God will wait until you land in a place that you thought was your ultimate destination, and He will create unexpected layovers just to show you all of what your new elevated life involves.

Although this divine dynamic may seem unusual to you, it is actually typical of God. He loves to use the element of surprise to show us how Godly He is, while reminding us how human we are. If we allow these elevated layovers to take their course, we will not only grow from them, but we will also go from them with a greater understanding on how our elevated lives become conduits through which others can experience NexLevel living.

Your Elevation Involves Desolation

Before you ascribe to the negative connotations of what your idea of desolation may be, let me preface this by explaining to you that your new elevated life has more to do with how you're positioned to bless others, rather than how God is positioned to bless you. The fact that you're in an elevated place already authenticates your blessings. It is all about how God wants to use you to be a blessing to those that come into contact with you. Some may call this "blessings by association". The Bible reveals that God personally took Ezekiel to a place called the valley of dry bones. The primary purpose of this trip was for God to show His Prophet the condition of His people. Upon their arrival, Ezekiel observes unprecedented desolation.

Desolation is defined as something that is barren, deprived, devastated, and uninhabitable. Then God asked him the critical question, "Can these bones live"? In other words, what do you think I'm capable of doing, not just for you, but through you? I really believe that this is the same question God is asking every NexLevel thinker because the issue is never Him getting the blessing to you, it's always Him getting the blessing through you. God is eager to take your obedience in the valley and use it as a springboard to bring others into the blessings of victory.

The involvement of desolation in your place of elevation is simply God's way of creating enough empathy and compassion in your heart, so you will dedicate your life to pull others up with your hands. Ezekiel replied "Lord, you know" and God said now that you know, that I know, let me show you what I'm capable of doing for you and through you.

Your Elevation Involves Illustration

I'm really convinced that God uses the involvement of illustration to not only teach you how He flows, but to also teach you how to flow. The word illustration means to furnish with drawings, pictures, and artwork intended for explanation. This is such a fascinating experience because God takes the spoken words Ezekiel released with his mouth and connected them to the strategic works of His Hands. In other words, God shows Ezekiel an illustration of how to build a body with bones.

At this point in your new elevated life you have to learn to take the bones of your finances, your marriage, your ministry, your health, your community, your family, your self-worth, your education, your job, your career, your idea, your invention, and let God show you how to build a body around it. When God shows you what He intends to do for you and through you, you are obligated to speak that over your life and cooperate with Him until He brings it into existence. Everybody or "every body" is made up of bones, flesh, skin, and breath. That means "every body" or area of your life requires certain fundamental elements and nutrients for its existence. You can't neglect a body or an area of your life and expect it to live. This was a valuable lesson that Ezekiel learned. Once he began to speak the word and work the word over the dead dry bones, he started seeing the broken pieces of a life that once existed, come back together again. I think it's very important for me to pause and prophetically insert this word to you:

No matter what area of your life it is that seems to be full of dead dry bones, all it takes is one word from God and He will bring that thing back together again! As a matter of fact, everything you went through in desolation that was designed to burden you and break you, God is using in illustration to bless you and to build you into a new elevated body that will house everything you need on your way to the NexLevel!

Your Elevation Involves Realization

In order for there to be a true realization, something has to be converted, grasped and brought into existence. If you're ever going to live in the realization of your elevated place, you have to not only **believe that you can** but you have to **act like you are.** That means you have to grasp it, grip it, embrace it, and live in the true experience of it.

This can't just be an idea you have in your head that never actually shows up in your life. The involvement of realization requires you to put the living flesh of who you are around the bones of what God told you to do. Realization can be defined as forced manifestation. Which means, once the manifestation of something shows up in your life, it is then your responsibility to give it body and breath so it can permanently stay in your life. Just because God said you can have it, doesn't mean when you get it that you will automatically keep it. The sustainability of God's manifested promise in your life is dependent upon the prophetic words that come from your mouth and the works that come from your hands.

The Prophet Ezekiel concludes his experience of desolation, illustration, and realization by not only learning how God flows but also learning how to flow with God. This is by far one of the most important lessons you have to learn in order to understand the deeper depths of living from an elevated place. As Ezekiel prepared to leave his elevated place of layover lessons, all he saw was the realization or the forced manifestation of an exceedingly great army of bodies breathing, living, and standing on their feet. This is exactly what God intends for every area of your life to look like when you learn how he flows and how to flow with Him.

CHAPTER 4

THE ELEVATION OF AN EAGLE

Isaiah 40:31

But they that wait upon the Lord shall renew their strength; they shall mount up with wings of eagles; they shall run, and not be weary; and they shall walk, and not faint.

It seems to me that every time God brings you to an elevated place in any area of your life, that the process He chooses and uses to get you there always shapes a different aspect of your character. History has proven that right when you think you've arrived at your final place of purpose, you realize that God is just getting started. He almost never concerns Himself with consulting you about where He's deciding to take you.

To be honest, that's one of the most attractive things that I love about God, because only He can be sovereign enough to blind you, break you, and simultaneously bless you, while He elevates you to the NexLevel of your life. What's even more amazing about this is that He allows this process to produce a character that results in having the capacity to handle the "weight while you wait"! In fact, the people who don't mount up with wings, are the people who refused to grow up during the wait.

It's absolutely impossible for anyone to fly high with wings of eagles if they never get conditioned during the wait in the nest. The process of waiting on God while He's working on you is the nest that He uses to condition your character for experiencing the elevation of an eagle.

3 CHARACTERISTICS OF AN EAGLE

God used Prophet Isaiah to give a Prophetic depiction of how He characterized His chosen people. Despite centuries of disappointments and generations of disobedience, God never allowed His estimation of their elevation to be mischaracterized by their condition. It was actually a common and popular opinion in ancient Hebrew culture that characterized God's people as eagles. Unlike any other common creature with wings, the eagles were uniquely peculiar. Only an eagle could plunge itself into a raging sea just to cast off its old feathers.

When God introduces you to your new elevated place, you must assume the characteristics of an eagle. That means you must accept the fact that the popular opinions of people who see you, will always try to mischaracterize you. Perhaps the common words they use to describe you won't be "uniquely peculiar". Instead they will use words like stuck up, selective, funny acting, a loner, introverted, unpredictable, weird, extra, or strange. When these things occur with common people who will never be able to elevate up to your level, just adopt the attitude of an eagle and plunge yourself in the reality of your elevated place of NexLevel Living!

1. The Eye of an Eagle

This is the characteristic that speaks to your vision, velocity, and victory. Each component that makes up this characteristic is essential to the elevation of an eagle. Vision refers to the visual value that comes from seeing beyond your natural sight. This level of insight gives you access to divine intelligence. The Bible clearly suggests that what you don't see will destroy you. Therefore, it is important to adopt the eye of an eagle through the first component of vision.

Velocity refers to the ability to move swiftly without interruptions. This ability always keeps you up to speed with what God is doing. Velocity enables you to stay sensitive to the move of God so you never miss or skip a season of manifestation. Victory is not just "something" but it's also "someone". When you adopt the eye of an eagle, you don't just claim your victory, you become the very example of victory.

Studies show that eagles have the ability to see miles out beyond their current space and speed. It's also understood that eagles don't eat dead things. Instead they wait and remain focused on fresh prey no matter how desperate they become or difficult the process may be. I believe that this characterization encompasses the vision, velocity, and victory we should all adopt in every area of our lives. When God elevates your life to the NexLevel, you have absolutely no reason to compromise your character because of moments of desperation and difficulty.

2. The Try of an Eagle

This is the characteristic that speaks to your diligence, discipline, and discomfort. Most of the things you experience in your elevated life are divinely designed to propel you into the NexLevel God has for you. God certainly doesn't withhold all the many blessed breaks in-between these transitional seasons. However, He always orchestrates opportunities to make you better and to take you higher.

Diligence refers to the constant effort to accomplish something. Which suggests that God will never be satisfied with NexLevel thinkers living mediocre lives. Your access to Elevation for NexLevel living demands that you always abound in daily efforts to become a better version of you, so you can live a better version of life. Discipline refers to the exercise, activity, regimen, and training that improves your skills. In order to adopt the "Try of an Eagle", you must understand that all healthy things grow, all growing things change, and all changing things challenge. If there is no challenge, there won't be change.

Discomfort is the indication in your nest that it's time for Elevation to your Nexlevel. At this stage of the elevation of an eagle the mother makes the nest uncomfortable. She takes the sticks and thorns that were previously hidden from the young eagle and points them at the young eagle. As long as the young eagle remained in the comfort of what it was used to, it would never step out on the edge to give life a try. This concept is called "stirring up the eagle's nest". How often does God have to make things uncomfortable in our life? He releases us into business, but we remain on the job. He instructs us to move, but we remind Him we're broke.

He shows you the building, but you show Him your budget. He gives you the idea, but you give Him an excuse. Once your process of waiting is over, God will kick you out of the nest of comfort and He will not allow you to remain in a compromised context that facilitates disobedience. The best choice for you is to step out on the edge, take that leap of faith, and let the wings work in the wind.

3. The Fly of an Eagle

This is the characteristic that speaks to your "will", warfare, and worship. At this elevated level of your life, you are able to prove what your character is made of. There are so many people who skipped the necessary process to get to this point and subsequently set themselves back because they didn't have the vision or the discipline to fly this high. Your "will" describes your arrival at a mature place in life that empowers you to take ownership of your own actions. This is where God separates birds from eagles. You are now ready to take on anything alone because you now possess the internal capacity to "will" yourself in and through it all.

Your warfare describes your aggressive nature to assert yourself in a way that keeps you on the offense instead of retreating to defense. The Prophet Isaiah mentioned running and walking which was not a natural, but a spiritual reference to the bold, flat footed authority you must assume when you adopt the characteristics of an eagle. Your worship describes the sacred space that God elevates you to, when you make the decision to fly like an eagle. Every stroke of your wing in worship continues to mount you up for that Elevation to the NexLevel.

The eagle is the only creature that has the strength, stamina, and stride to fly into the storm without suffering life threatening injuries. As a matter of fact, the stronger the wind, the higher they rise because they use the speed and strength of the wind to take them closer to the sun. There is absolutely nothing you will set out to do at this level in your life that will flop, fold, or fail. God's blessings for you will be manifested in every dream, desire, vision, idea, conception, invention, plan, or opportunity that you choose to pursue. What an extraordinary experience it is to have the eye, the try, & the fly of an eagle that characterizes how God elevates His people into NexLevel living.

CHAPTER 5

MAY THE FORCE BE WITH YOU

Isaiah 59:17, 19

For the Lord put on righteousness as a breastplate, salvation as a helmet, garments as clothing. When the enemy comes in like a flood, the Lord will lift up a standard against him.

At this point in your quest to increase your capacity for Elevation to the NexLevel, it is important that you become very emphatic with your words and deliberate in your deeds. Without this daily discipline and disposition, you will run the risk of descending back down to ground level thinking. Whether it's a relationship, a job offer, an application for a loan, a ministry move, a community project, or a business deal, you must be poised to project the power you possess as a NexLevel thinker.

According to Prophet Isaiah, Israel's procrastination leads them to passivity. Instead of aggressively pursuing their NexLevel in God, they chose to allow their mental conditioning to rob them of their heavenly positioning. As a consequence, God gave them over to their opposition and they suffered, having to live their lives under the very people they were instructed to be over. In other words, they never elevated their minds for NexLevel living.

Now before you smirk or suggest that this should've been a no brainer for them, please keep in mind that God was infiltrating their opposition and literally using their opposers as a rod of anger to spank Israel for their previous acts of disobedience. This is exactly why no matter how high you go up in any area of your life, you have to remain humble under the mighty hand of God. Nothing or no one should be more important in your life than your personal relationship and elevation with God. If this covenantal rule is ever breached or broken, then you will literally force God's hand to subject you to a spanking.

The problem is you don't know who or what He chooses to use in order to spank you back into humble submission. For some people this sounds judgmental and detrimental to characterize such a loving God like this, but the Bible clearly says that who God loves, He chastens. The word chasten carries the idea of inflicting pain for the purpose of improvement. This suggests that God never intended to harm Israel, He was intentionally helping Israel develop the tolerance they would need in order for them to push past the pain of their problems and be propelled into the elevated place of their purpose.

My question to you is this: What situational pain are you facing right now? My challenge is for you to recognize that not only is it working together for your good, but recognize that it's working for the purpose to make you better! Once you recognize this, you'll be able to realize that who God chooses to bruise the most, He ultimately chooses to use the most. This recognition and realization became a conditional complication for Israel. So God sent Isaiah to save the day.

Unfortunately for those who wanted to end their process

prematurely, Isaiah didn't compromise for the crowd. In no uncertain terms, his prophetic word indicated that in order for Israel to take it by force, they had to learn to tolerate force.

Your Elevation Forces Customization

Customization describes the molding or building according to individual or personal specifications. Whenever God customizes your life, He makes sure that everyone and everything in it fits your life perfectly. God seems to be very particular about who He wants in your life and what He wants for your life. Which is why you have to exercise extreme caution when it comes to who and what you welcome to connect with you.

There has to be an exclusivity to your elevation. Your position in life, in ministry, in business, in school, in the workplace, or in the world, can't be a copy-cat, a cookie-cut, or a copy and paste of someone else. You have to be ok with being uniquely you. When you are, everyone you bring in your life and everything you do in your life, will perfectly fit your personality and flawlessly match your prophetic make-up. At this elevated level in life, you will never have to squeeze squares into your circle!

If you noticed in the Biblical text, Isaiah reveals that the Savior was perfectly fit, not just for the fight He faced in the now, but also for the favor Israel would find for themselves in the NexLevel. The implication to that is this, even if you're satisfied with where you are in the progressive success of your Elevation to the NexLevel, you should be selfishly unselfish enough to clothe yourself with the care and concern of the welfare of others.

Sometimes your Elevation in life is God's way of putting you in a position so He can work through you in order to shift the social-economic structure of a community and ultimately push a culture forward. I believe that there's an epidemic of no-level bottom feeders who's only job is to force you out of your elevated place of favor so you will be hindered in helping others experience NexLevel living.

If I'm correct, that means you should assume more of a responsibility to have a heightened awareness of who or what is in your circle. By doing this, you will avoid the poison of their "stinking thinking" from entering in your elevated mind. You will also refute the notion of no-level bottom feeders, that people have no choice but to subject themselves to situational conditions that don't reflect God's best for their lives.

Your Elevation Forces Confrontation

Confrontation describes the act of defiance and deliberate hostility. It carries the idea of standing in front of or in the face of anything that opposes what you know to be true. Now that God has fit you for the fight, you should have the backbone to deal with all the bondage around you. You should be confident, clear, and bold about not allowing anything in your life that opposes what you know to be true about your Elevation to the NexLevel.

If you want everything you set your heart and hands to do to prosper for you, then you should have the backbone to believe and behave like you know this to be true. Anytime God allows confrontation in your life, He's totally confident in your commitment to be bold about what you believe. That is why your confrontation is forced, because God forces you to force the cons out of your life. These cons can be people, places, and things that are designed to obstruct your view and oppose your navigation while you're on your way to the NexLevel.

The New Testament suggests that Kingdom minded, NexLevel thinkers know exactly how to "take it by force". This type of force doesn't mean you're disrespectfully bullying people and taking something that's not yours. This type of force actually means that you are extremely confident about who you are, who's you are, where you are, and what you have access to. This confidence is what gives you the backbone and boldness to be very clear about what you will and will not tolerate in your NexLevel life. So instead of taking some things from people, you receive everything from God because your NexLevel life has granted you access to open heaven favors and blessings.

It's absolutely imperative for you to keep in mind that your confrontation has allowed you to separate the pros from the cons. This separation requires clear defined roles for everyone and everything that connects to you. The Bible demands that we "come out from among them and be separated". Which means that you must be definitive in distinguishing the favored from the frauds. If people can't think like you most likely they can't live like you. You never want to become a magnet for maggots and cause your good to be evil spoken of.

Now let me be very clear because I don't want you to assume that I'm suggesting you can't have family and friends in your Nexlevel life. I'm just saying that you have to be mature enough to differentiate the people you live in the blessing with, from the people you're just called to be a blessing to. This is how you always avoid unnecessary hate and ungodly confrontation. Remember, when you have acquired a distaste for poverty and a true taste for prosperity, you will offend people who still have a sour taste in their minds mouth about NexLevel living!

Your Elevation Forces Contextualization

Contextualization describes the process of bringing things into one central location. This is God's way of helping you make sense of what you went through to get to where you are in life. In reality, God used your previous process as a case study to authenticate His authority. He knew that the deliverance from your struggles would be used as a success story to many. When God contextualizes your life, He brings every piece of the prophetic puzzle of His promises into a sacred space called "The NexLevel".

This sacred space is exclusive to you and tailor made for you. It encompasses the full protective services that heaven provides, so you can live drama free in the promises he made to you. For some, this contextualization is revealed in how He brings their family back together again. For others, it is seen in how God puts them back on their financial feet. Whatever process you had to go through in order to be right where you are, I believe that God is finalizing your process and contextualizing your life.

Even if we have a different process, we all share the same promise that *"when the enemy comes in like a flood, The Lord will lift up a standard against him"*. In other words, God will contextualize every area of your life and bring you into a sacred space for Elevation to the NexLevel!

CHAPTER 6

WELCOME TO THE NEXLEVEL

Romans 5:2

Through Him also we have our access, entrance, and introduction by faith into this grace or state of God's favor in which we firmly and safely stand.

Since your belief, behavior, and boldness has now given you the backbone to experience the totality of an elevated life, it's important for you to familiarize yourself with the practical purpose of your new platform. I'm simply amazed at how many people have become philosophers of grace, but never transitioned into practitioners of grace. I believe that this partial presentation of grace comes from a fragmented definition and description of what grace is, and how grace works.

Grace can be defined as the unmerited favor of God. Grace can be described as God's way of doing us a favor that we can never be good enough to repay Him. In fact, Ephesians 2:8 says *"we are saved by grace, through faith, which is not from yourselves but it is the gift from God"*. So the misunderstanding and misappropriation of grace is not about your "Salvation", it's all about your "Elevation". The reason for this is because the concept of favor comes from grace and it is built on the basis of what God freely does for you, now that He's saved you.

I want to preface the details of my next discussion by being unequivocally bold and Biblically sound about the fact that, if you've never experienced God's "Amazing Grace" in "Salvation", you can't enjoy God's "Fabulous Favor" in "Elevation".

The truth is that there is no other name by which you can be "Saved by Grace" and favored by God, than the name of Jesus Christ! From a theological perspective, the Book of Romans is considered the Constitution of Christianity that the Apostle Paul used to defend his philosophy or his values and views concerning the religious practice of the Christian faith.

The reason why this is very important for you to know is because your practice of something is dependent upon your philosophy of something. If you don't possess the proper philosophy or values and views about Grace, you probably won't practice a prosperous life of favor. Once you understand that Grace is for Salvation and Favor is for Elevation, then you can begin to live a favorable life in the NexLevel.

What is the NexLevel?

The NexLevel can be defined as the supernatural experience of elevated advances without limitations. This is not just a place you "go to", but is also a space you "flow from". The process you went through for elevation, is what God used to qualify you for this experience. If you were never qualified for elevation, you would have never been verified to have access to the NexLevel. Now that you have access to this NexLevel, you have to build your practice around this philosophy. That means you have to embrace the grace to level-up, learn-up, and live-up!

Embrace The Grace To Level-Up

In order to embrace the grace to level-up, you must take your life from justified to verified. This experience requires you to fully grasp the fact that you're destined to live a NexLevel life, from the top down, not from the bottom up. Despite what your circumstances look like in the circumference of your life, you are the head and not the tail, you are above and not beneath, you are the lender, not the borrower, blessed, not cursed, and because you are verified, God has favored the works of your hands!

In Romans 5:1, the Apostle Paul emphatically defends his values and views by challenging the readers to embrace the grace to level-up. His belief was that *"since we are justified and acquitted by grace through faith, then let us grasp the fact that we have peace and joy with God"*.

The Hebrew word for peace here is *"Shalom"*, which means harmony, wholeness, prosperity, and tranquility. Shalom encompasses a blessed experience in spirit, soul, and body. It also carries the idea that there is absolutely nothing favorable missing, lacking, lost, or left out of your life.

Having peace and joy with God doesn't mean you're exempt

from pain and problems, it just means that you choose not to participate in the pitiful exchange of pain and problems. That is why your challenge to embrace the grace to level-up should provoke you to get a grip on enjoying peace and joy with God since He's verified your NexLevel Life.

Embrace The Grace To Learn-Up

In order to embrace the grace to learn-up, you must take your life from verified to certified. This experience requires you to enter into new territories of teaching and transparency. The expansion of your experience should produce the advancement of your intelligence. I say this respectfully, but the truth is that I've met countless people who were educated but who had no sense of intelligence. When you're educated, you have been informed, taught, and have developed the faculties for a particular subject.

When you're intelligent, you have the intuitive capacity for learning, reasoning, and grasping truths with or without a formal education. You may have heard it said that some people have book smarts, but others have street smarts. Learning-Up is not about reading truth from a book, it's all about living the truth in your life. I'm convinced that spiritual, mental, emotional, and financial intelligence will always allow you to experience NexLevel living, and afford you access to be on the cutting-edge above the rest. Education alone may work on paper, but true intelligence will produce in practice.

Embrace The Grace To Live-Up

In order to embrace the grace to live-up, you must take your life from certified to glorified. This experience requires you to leave the natural realm of philosopher and access the supernatural dimension of practitioner. Very few people understand the power of their practice. We are so programmed to believe what people say, that we hardly see what people do.

When you become a supernatural practitioner, you receive unlimited jurisdiction from God that gives you a legal right to enter any sphere of influence. Once you're in, you are now able to start your practice as an expert on favor. That means, because God has given you favor, you in turn become a conduit through which someone else can be favored. Whether it's a seed you sow, a deed you perform, a job you do, a family you bless, a church you serve, a door you open, or just a smile you give, you are operating in the unlimited jurisdiction of a favor practitioner.

When you are Living-Up in this high dimensional frequency of favor, you understand that everything you need to see in your personal life becomes a reflection of what you sowed and showed others in your public life. This is the very essence of being more blessed to give than to receive. Furthermore, a true practitioner never expends their time philosophically telling people what they should do, they just practically show people how it's done!

CHAPTER 7

3 C'S TO NEXLEVEL LIVING

1 Corinthians 15:58

Therefore, my beloved brethren, be steadfast, immovable, always abounding in the work of the Lord, knowing that your Labor in the Lord is not in vain.

It should be apparent to you by now that your Elevation to the NexLevel involves lots of leveling, learning, and living. One of the reasons why this is much more complex than what most philosophers will be honest to tell you, is because it demands action and attention every day. If you begin this journey with a sprinters mentality, you will gas out real fast and give up too soon. Longevity in the NexLevel can only be accomplished when you embrace a marathon mentality.

King Solomon said it best in the Book of Ecclesiastes that *"the race is not always given to the swift, nor the battle given to the strong, but time and chance are given to both"*. What's fascinating about this is that his wisdom expresses life like a race and a battle. This is a very important part of your Elevation to the NexLevel because life is not about existing, it's all about living. If you're not using your time to live, you're chancing your life until you die.

When you identify with what you need to live with longevity in the NexLevel, you lower your chances to die. Of course I'm not referring to the inevitability of your natural death, I'm referring to the possibility of your potential's death.

51

1. You Need Conviction

A conviction is a fixed and firm belief that someone possess in who they are, who's they are, what they have, and where they're going. Your conviction is what keeps you grounded in truth, even when your life starts voicing its opinions. In law, a conviction is the verdict that results when a court finds someone guilty for something for which they were accused.

When it comes to your NexLevel, there should be no doubt about what you believe God wants to do for you and where you believe He wants to take you. If business deals go bad, your conviction must be good. If relationships break, your conviction holds you together. If you're denied the loan, your conviction is still approved. If things are not moving up, your conviction never hits the ground. This fixed and firm belief has to be embedded in the core of your character in order to sustain you when the accusations of not enough, and the prosecutions of just enough come against you. God has charged you with NexLevel living and He's found you guilty for more than enough!

2. You Need Commitment

A commitment is a permanent pledge to a position on an issue or idea. Your commitment is what binds you and subsequently brings you to the NexLevel blessings God has built for you. If you don't establish a conviction, you won't sustain a commitment, because your commitment needs a basis of belief to be built on.

People who waver in their faith may have established some sort of belief at some point in their pursuit of whatever their NexLevel was. The problem is that they forgot to put a pledge on the basis of their belief. One of the most important questions ever asked in the Bible is, *"who hindered you"?* Think about the magnitude of how the hindrances of the human heart, can keep you from experiencing your best life.

In 1 Corinthians 15:58, the Apostle Paul uses a critical word that relates to your need for commitment. He establishes the fact that as convicted believers we are charged to be steadfast and immovable. The words steadfast and immovable are both compound words that are commonly used to identify a fixed, firm belief and behavior. They also carry the idea of being strong and steady in faith. This suggests that your conviction concerning your NexLevel Living will always keep you steady and strong in faith, as long as you build your commitment on the basis of it.

3. You Need Consistency

A consistency is a degree of determination that constitutes longevity in something you do. Your consistency is what creates the constitution that preserves the integrity of your conviction and commitment. Written within the framework of this constitution is the truth of God's promises about your NexLevel Living. All groups, governing bodies, corporations, and the like, are subject to the principles and powers of the constitution. This is exactly what your consistency provides for you in every area of life. The basis of your conviction and the binding of your commitment is revealed in your responsibility to Live-Up to the standard or the constitution of consistency. According to the final clause in 1 Corinthians 15:58, the Apostle Paul urges all convicted, committed believers to always abound in the work of the Lord, knowing that our labor in the Lord is not in vain.

The phrase "always abound" denotes a daily discipline of eager execution. Which means, you never let up on what you're called to do until your legacy is permanently established for you. It's important to note that your legacy is tied to your longevity, your longevity is tied to your integrity, and your integrity is tied to your character. Your character, however, can only be birthed from your consistency in the conviction and commitment you possess concerning your NexLevel Living!

CHAPTER 8

NEXLEVEL EXPECTATIONS

Genesis 26:22

He went from there and dug yet another well, but there was no fighting over this one, so he named it wide-open spaces. Saying now God has given us plenty of space so we can be fruitful in the land.

Studies show that most people think about wealth, health, and their family's well-being on a daily basis. Some of these studies also show that most of these people will openly admit to having a deep seated desire to experience freedom and fulfillment in these sentimental areas. What most of these studies don't show, however, is how disappointingly difficult it is for the average person to experience true freedom and fulfilment in any area of their life. One of the primary reasons for this omission of information, is the fact that unrealistic expectations are easy to sell. What I mean by that is some people want to know how to live on top, but they refuse to set the proper expectations while they're on the bottom.

If you don't know what to expect when God takes you to the top, you will fail miserably and eventually hit rock bottom. That is why no one should be over ambitious to experience NexLevel Living until they count up the cost by setting the proper expectations. If this is where you are, I want you to begin this process by doing everything you can to demonstrate your deep seated desire for NexLevel Wealth, Health, and Living for you and your family! Now that you understand how important it is to set the proper NexLevel expectations, I believe it is equally important to know what each NexLevel expectation is and how you must integrate them in your life.

In my personal experience as a Pastor, Entrepreneur, and Social Economic Strategist, I have identified with 3 things you should expect when God brings you to the NexLevel. Please keep in mind, when I say NexLevel, I'm simply referring to your supernatural experience of elevated advances without limitations. My definition and description of what the NexLevel is and how the NexLevel works, should never be limited to one particular category. As a matter of fact, "The NexLevel" is literally encompassed by our God, *"who is able to do exceedingly, superabundantly, multiplied more than all you dare ask or think, according to His power that is working in you"*!

You Should Expect Problems

A problem is defined as a situation proposed for solution that needs attention. The purpose of a problem is to teach you how to take your mind off the issues around you and tap into the answers within you. That is why your expectation of the problem will give you a competitive advantage over the problem. If you always avoid problems, you will never set proper expectations to solve them. This lack of responsibility and awareness will cause you to become the very problem you should have solved.

The Bible reveals in Genesis 26, that there was a famine in

Isaac's promise land. Although Isaac was the child of the promised blessing, he still realized that he had a problem. After consulting God on how to deal with the problem, he received a strategic solution. As he implemented his strategy in digging new wells of wealth, the local herdsmen began to quarrel with him and take claim of what he started producing.

Instead of magnifying the problem by defending his position, he decided to leave them there and move to another well of wealth. This is a very important lesson because when you set the proper expectations for pending problems, God will give you strategic solutions that you can implement to make provision for your NexLevel Living.

You Should Expect Pressure

Pressure is defined as the exertion of force that is caused by the weight upon a surface by a foreign object. The purpose of pressure is to create a constant demand for something to keep moving with momentum. Almost every day of my life I'm bombarded by people who constantly say that they want to go to the NexLevel. Some of these people want it for their health, their finances, and even for their children. Others want the NexLevel for their ministries, their churches, and even for their businesses.

Unfortunately for many of these precious people, they just can't handle the pressure. There is no other way for me to articulate this sobering truth other than saying, the demand for NexLevel Living is just too much. Let me be very clear because this pressure and demand is not about what's coming against you from the outside, it's actually about what's unwilling to grow up in you from the inside. If you notice in Genesis 26, everywhere Isaac went to dig a new well of wealth, there were people patiently waiting there, ready to stop him from receiving the provision for his NexLevel Living. He never lost his cool and he never compromised his position as the child of the promised blessing. In fact, Isaac was so convinced and confident that the blessing of Abraham was on his life that he was excited about being a blessing to those who secretly wanted to pronounce a curse upon him. He also knew that the pressure was creating a greater demand to keep him moving toward his promise. My critical question is, what problems and pressures have you been avoiding? I want to challenge you to not only embrace them but learn to get comfortable living with them. If you're unwilling to see it, you're unworthy to solve it!

You Should Expect Plenty

Plenty is defined as a large, sufficient, sustainable amount of something that's been in demand. The purpose of plenty is to overwhelm you with more than enough, until it makes your current space seem small and uncomfortable. Most of the people who make it to the place of plenty seem to share one common theme. They have all become what I call "selfishly unselfish". Now, as bad as that statement may sound, it's actually an amazing compliment to them. When someone is selfishly unselfish, that means they have engineered their lives in a way to create this extreme obsession for more, not just for the purpose of having more, but for the purpose of helping more. I know it can be difficult to understand, but if you ever elevate your mind to embrace that place, it will absolutely change your life! Just in case you're still wrestling with this notion of being selfishly unselfish, let me validate my view by suggesting to you that out of over 7.5 billion people on the planet, only a little over 2 billion are professing Christians. That means that there are people who need to be saved, children who need to be adopted, families that need to be supported, communities that need to be restored, and nations that need to be built.

These facts support the same promises that God made to Isaac in Genesis 26, when He said that *"I will bless you, multiply you, make your name great, and bring you into a place of plenty"*. As a result of Isaac's obedience to set the proper expectations for problems and pressure, the Bible says that he called his next well "the place of plenty". As believers, we should always be willing to open ourselves up to the possibilities of being selfishly unselfish, in a deliberate attempt to take the attention and resources from our problems and pressures, and bring God's people into a place of plenty.

CHAPTER 9

LIVING IN THE NEXLEVEL

Deuteronomy 2:3

Then God said, you have roamed around this mountain long enough: turn upward.

Getting comfortable with a certain routine in life is much easier than most people are willing to admit. Since we are creatures of habit we don't always mind doing the same things the same way. Everyday people all over the world wake up to the same routine. They pray, they eat, they shower, they do their hair, they shave, and they prepare to complete another day.

Whether it's school, work, business, or church, the perpetuation of these same cycles seem to plague every human being. What I find fascinating about this idea of regimented routines, is that God seems to be uninterested in ascribing to these so-called daily disciplines that we tend to form a romantic relationship with.

Surveys show that any one habit can possibly be broken and any new habit can potentially be formed within any 21 to 30-day period. I guess this explains why God was very specific and emphatic in directing Moses and Israel through the wilderness. What was meant to be a 2 to 3-week journey, turned into a 40-year nightmare. One of the primary reasons for this extreme delay was not just their blatant disobedience, but I attribute some of this delay to their unwillingness to break bad habits.

There is absolutely no human way that over 2 million people were unable to navigate their way out of the wilderness. As unbelievable as it sounds, this is exactly what occurred. The truth is that whenever you romanticize with the ideals you set in your mind about doing the same things the same way, you will become blinded by the regimen of your own routines. Living In The NexLevel requires a sensitivity and a pliability that keeps you flexible enough to not only move when God moves, but to also move how God moves. In order for your faith to move with this level of flexibility, there are 3 things you must be willing to do.

1. You Must Be Willing To Address Your Limitations

Addressing your limitations allows you to permanently remove everything that holds you in a context that has become too small for you. The operative word here is "address", which not only carries the idea of what you say, but also for where you go. When you address your limitations, you literally tell the current context of small places that it's time to go.

Too many people today are stuck being bottle-necked or capped-off in small places that no longer fit the framework of their faith. If they don't choose to make a move, they will be forced to tap-out and subsequently settle into a small place of mediocrity. Some of these places may mean a lot to you, but they hardly mean anything to God because He knows that if you stay in small too long, it will shrink your mind down to its size. You can't just pray away your limitations, you must learn to walk away from your limitations. That is why in Deuteronomy 2:3, God stops Moses in his tracks. At this point, Moses was comfortably uncomfortable living in the regimented routine of doing the same things, the same way. I want to caution you not to be so inconclusive in your premature assessment of why Moses was so slow to make a move. In fact, you should take a sneak peek into every area of your life, just to see where you may be stuck in a current context of small places. Whether you admit it or not, everybody suffers from this habitual practice at different junctures of their life. There are so many things that you have to factor into the equation of why you are still stuck in the now and so slow to move to the next.

Some of the things that cause this to happen to you are not always bad, they're actually good. Which means that good things have the propensity to go bad! It can be the "good thing" of your marriage, your family, your job, your degree, your education, your health, your mind, your spirituality, your church, your vision, your car, your house, your dreams, your goals, and most certainly, your finances.

2. You Must Be Willing To Adjust Your Situation

Adjusting your situation allows you to change things around you so that they fit, conform, and adapt to you. The operative word here is "adjust", which carries the idea of adding or joining something along side. When you adjust your situation, you literally take whatever God has placed at your disposal and use it as motivation to make a bigger move. This doesn't imply that you will change your situation, this implies that you will adjust your situation.

Don't become so romantic with the idea of changing things, that you divorce the reality for adjusting things. You have to accept the fact that there are some people and things that may never change "for you", but they can all be adjusted "by you". Assuming the responsibility for the proper placement of people and things in your life, is one of the greatest adjustments you will ever make. This is how to take inventory of who's just with you and who's really for you. Most of the good people and things in your life that subsequently go bad, are the people and things that you stop taking inventory of. You have to be very intentional on checking in and checking up, otherwise you run the risk of people and things checking out!

3. You Must Be Willing To Accept Your Escalation

Accepting your escalation allows you to scale your speed to a pace that causes your small place to disappear on impact. The operative word here is "accept", which denotes a consensual agreement between a giver and a receiver. When you accept your escalation, you literally shift the gears of your mind and activate the motivational motor of your life. During this critical moment, you have to trust the transmission of the revelation that God gives to you concerning the greater places He's about to take you. This is very significant to Living In

The NexLevel, because you will never be able to scale pass the pace of your obedience. If you noticed in Deuteronomy 2:3, once God stops Moses and gets his attention, he says, *"you have roamed or cruised around this mountain or small place long enough"*. In other words, where you are right now is tired of you, but where you're about to go is tailor made for you!

He then concretizes His heavenly conversation with just two words, *"Turn-Upward"!* Simply put, God did not want Moses to perpetuate the same cycle of regimented routines. This was the moment that Moses had to maximize by refusing to look down at his limitations, refusing to look out at his situation, and choosing to turn-up in his escalation! My critical question to you is, what's stopping you from "Turning-Up"? You must be willing to hit the acceleration for Elevation to the NexLevel!

CHAPTER 10

MAINTAINING A NEXLEVEL LIFESTYLE

Numbers 13:30

Then Caleb quieted the people before Moses, and said, let us go up at once and take possession of it; for we will certainly conquer it.

Whenever there's a demand to make a major move in your life, it typically requires extended amounts of time before you decide on what you're going to do. The reason for this is because most people are responsible enough to do their due diligence before they make a permanent decision. This is not an unusual process for making major moves, especially since contemplation, deliberation, reflection, and anticipation all take time. This only becomes an issue when you have completed this thorough process, but you are still uncertain about your decision to make a move. Sometimes people can get so hung up on the intricate details of their decisions, that they contract this debilitating disease called "the paralysis of analysis". This disease can have long term affects that keep you living in pauses, but never getting to promises.

In fact, one of the signs of this disease is the tendency to enjoy temporary experiences of NexLevel Living, without ever taking your NexLevel experiences and turning them into a NexLevel Lifestyle! There is a fundamental difference between a life experience and a lifestyle. A life experience is something that you participate in and gain knowledge from. Just because you have an experience in something, doesn't necessarily mean you will make a lifestyle of something. This is exactly why it is so easy for someone to know history, but it's much more difficult for someone to make history. A lifestyle describes the experiences, tastes, habits, attitudes, and subsequent standards that constitute a mode of living. This word carries the idea of someone developing a permanent mode of operation, or what we commonly refer to as an "M.O.". People who study history like to use the idea of an M.O., in order to examine the identity and determine the actions of who certain history makers were, and what their historical lives were about. In other words, they don't just look at someone's single life experience, they also look into the sum total of that person's lifestyle.

If you are at the point in your life where you are now ready to take your temporary experiences of NexLevel Living and turn them into your NexLevel Lifestyle, you are exactly where God wants you to be. It's important to note, however, that once you make the move to get there, you have to maintain the mode to stay there. In order to maintain the mode for a NexLevel Lifestyle, you must remain faithful, focused, and fruitful.

You Must Remain Faithful

Faithfulness is defined as living up to God's expectations of you. The purpose of faith is to give you living proof that God told you to do something. This proof is what empowers you to fix any flaws and filter any fears that may pop up in your life. In Numbers 13, God instructs Moses to *"send men to spy out the promise land"*. This experience was God's way of showing Moses how to take Israel from temporary Godly experiences, into a permanent Godly lifestyle. For so long Israel enjoyed the appetizers of God's blessings of Manna. Now, God wanted to treat them to a lifetime of full course meals. In order for this to happen, God needed someone to prep the meal. One of the greatest travesties in a person's life, is for them to be satisfied snacking on the appetizers of what could've been for them, instead of feasting on the favor filled meals of what should've been for them. The tasting is designed to familiarize you with the trusting, but the trusting is what God uses to take you into a greater element of your NexLevel Lifestyle.

Notice how selective God was in who He chose to take the leap of faith and spy out the promise land. Out of the twelve men who tasted the temporary experience of the promise land, only two of them developed an appetite to turn it into a lifestyle. Despite the fact that the return ratio of the faithful few is relatively low, God still uses the infrastructure of our faith as a framework for the entire landscape of our NexLevel Promise Land.

You Must Remain Focused

Focus is defined as directing one's attention, attraction, and activity to a perceived point of interest. The purpose of focus is to cause whatever faith shows you, to come into view. Too many people want to receive the benefits of the fruit, without taking the necessary tests to be disciplined with the focus. This is why it's so important for your faithfulness to be established, because it becomes a solid foundation for your much needed focus. Once your focus is crystal clear, you will only pick things in your now, that you know have the potential to remain in your later. The Bible says in Numbers 13:27, when the twelve men returned to give their report about their temporary experience in the promise land, immediately ten of them begin to express their concerns.

Although they explained how this promised place was flowing and fruitful, they still showed clear signs that their faith was out of focus. What's disappointing about their report and response is, all they had to do was keep their attention, attraction, and activity on what their faith initially showed them. No matter what the enemy brings in your life in an attempt to obstruct your view, you must remain faithful and focused on what God showed you and told you to do.

You Must Remain Fruitful

Fruitfulness is defined as the profitable production of abundant growth. The purpose of fruitfulness is to bring you to your ultimate place of produced promises in your NexLevel Lifestyle. At this point in your life, God intends for you to become an expert at picking and producing fruit. As an expert in fruit, your faithful focus will give you precision for every pick. Whether you're picking a spouse, a car, a house, a business partner, a new location for your church, a community to serve, an idea, a vacation, a job, or a new hobby to pursue, your faithful focus will produce profitable fruit for you. This is the same productive fruitfulness that

Caleb possessed in Numbers 13:30. It was here that Caleb demanded every pathetic echo of fear to be quiet, so the true prophetic voice of faith could be heard. Now that he had the nation's attention, he said, *"let's all go up now, take the land, because I know we can do it"!*

I am absolutely positively convinced that everything you have been through in the process of your life, has brought you to this promised place. Now that you're here, it's time to come all the way up and take your place for Elevation to the NexLevel!

A PRAYER FOR

ELEVATION TO THE NEXLEVEL

Matthew 16:19

I will give you the keys (authority) of the Kingdom of Heaven; and whatever you bind, forbid, declare unlawful on earth will be the same in Heaven. Whatever you loose, permit, declare lawful on earth will be the same in Heaven.

Father God, in the name of The Lord Jesus, I decree and declare your prophetic promises for Elevation To The NexLevel over every area of my life. I take authority over and bind every demonic spirit on assignment to stop me from entering my NexLevel Life.

I exercise my dominion as a King and Priest in God, and I command the earth's resources to yield forth fruit to sustain me throughout my experience of NexLevel Living. I dispatch the Angels of The Lord and Ministering Spirits that are assigned to assist me in the continued success of my NexLevel objectives.

Lord, I thank you in advance for every miracle and favorable blessing you are releasing to me for my NexLevel Lifestyle. I receive it, believe it, and I say "it is so"! In the name of The Lord Jesus I pray, Amen.

ABOUT THE AUTHOR

Ramone Preston is recognized and respected as a revolutionary Prophet, Pastor, Entrepreneur, and Socio-Economic Strategist on a mission to empower people!

Throughout his tenure he's traveled, preached, consulted, and established countless ministries, businesses, community development programs and economic initiatives for individuals, churches, and entrepreneurs.

He currently serves as the Pastor and CEO of Kingdom Harvest Outreach Ministries and Ramone Preston Ministries. He also serves as the CEO of Ramone Preston Enterprises, LLC, which is a holding company and conglomerate for other businesses and investments.

Ramone and his beautiful wife, Dione Preston currently live in the Buckhead Community of Atlanta, Ga. and he's the proud Father (Papa) of two children, Ramani (Tai'lyn) and Ramone Preston Jr.

70009141R00044

Made in the USA
Middletown, DE
14 April 2018